1066

ILLUSTRATED BY CHRIS RUTH

Tarquin

To my husband who will always be my steadfast supporter.

Publisher's Note

1066 is the first of our series Big Stories for Little Historians.
We hope you enjoy the series, whether you are reading them yourself, or with children, or using them in the classroom.

Teachers may like to know that there is a Teacher Book available to extend the 1066 book, providing cross-curriculum resources and printable resources.

More details on this, and the series, can be found as www.bigstories.online

---

ISBN (book): 978-1-91356-539-8
ISBN (ebook): 978-1-91356-540-4
Design By Head Design
Printed in the UK

Published by Tarquin
Suite 74, 17 Holywell Hill
St Albans AL1 1DT
United Kingdom
info@tarquingroup.com
www.tarquingroup.com

The time is 1066, when people lived in small villages in wooden houses, with roofs made of straw. All the members of the same family would live together, often in just one room where they would sleep, wash and eat. People were farmers, and someone would always have the job of keeping the animals safe. There were wolves in Britain. A King called Edward was on the throne. His people were called the Anglo Saxons.

All was calm in England, but there would be an event so ground shaking, it would change England forever. Edward was a good King and spent a lot of his time praying. Edward had no children to take over the throne. When he died on a cold day in January 1066, no one knew who was going to be King. There was going to be a big argument. Edward had been a little silly. He had made promises to lots of different people that they could be King after him.

Four people wanted to be King of England. They wanted to be King to make them rich, powerful and be in charge of a big Kingdom. The four people were William of Normandy, Harald Hardrada, Harold Godwinson and Edgar Atheling. Each of the four people felt they should be King of England.

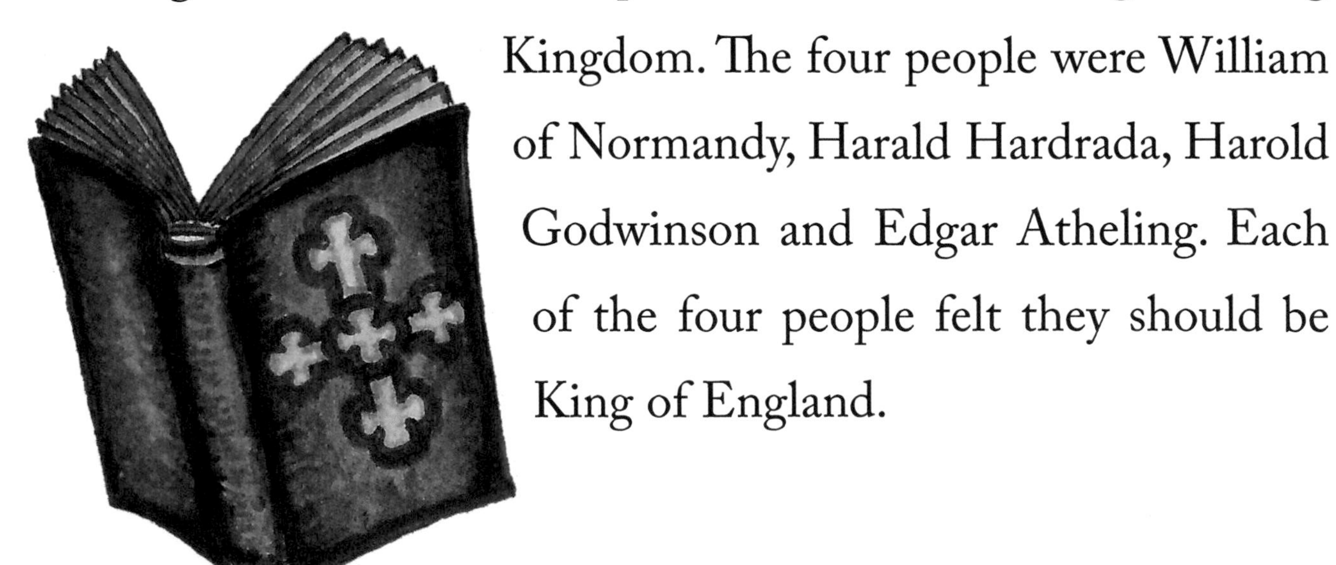

THE CONTENDERS
HAROLD
HARALD
EDGAR
WILLIAM

Firstly, Edward had promised the Throne to a man called William of Normandy. He was already a King in Normandy. William was a short man with a stumpy legs and not very handsome. He was very firm and often stood up for what he believed in. He said that Edward had promised he could be King one day. Edward had spent time as a child in Normandy where William was King, and they had become friends. Edward may even have sent a special message over to Normandy to tell William he would be the next king.

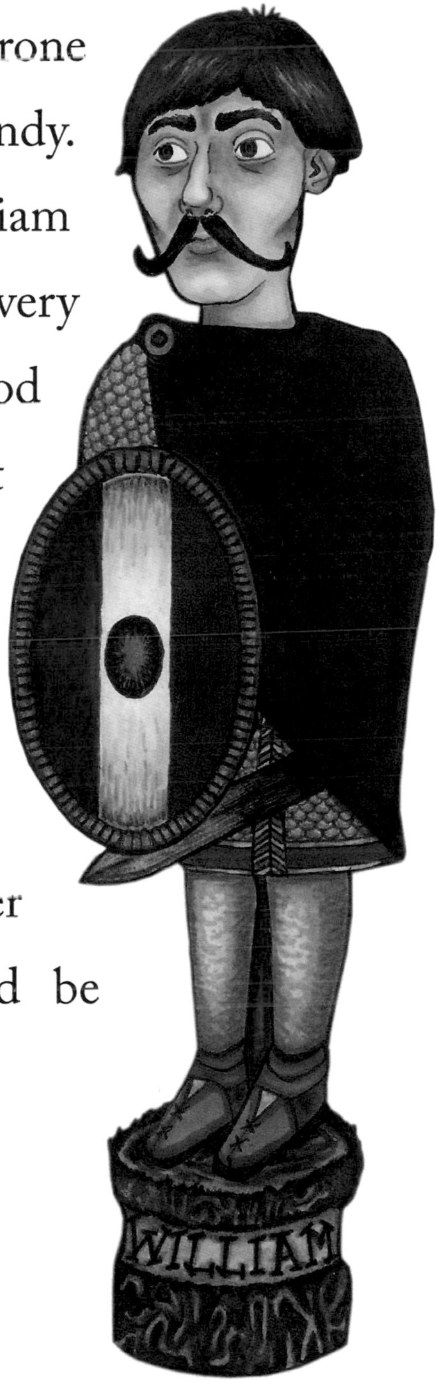

It would be a letter sent by ship from England. The ship carrying the letter was sadly shipwrecked and William helped save the men on the ship.

Dear William,
In thanks for your help in saving my men from their ship-wreck and your friend-ship, I name you as my successor.
Edward

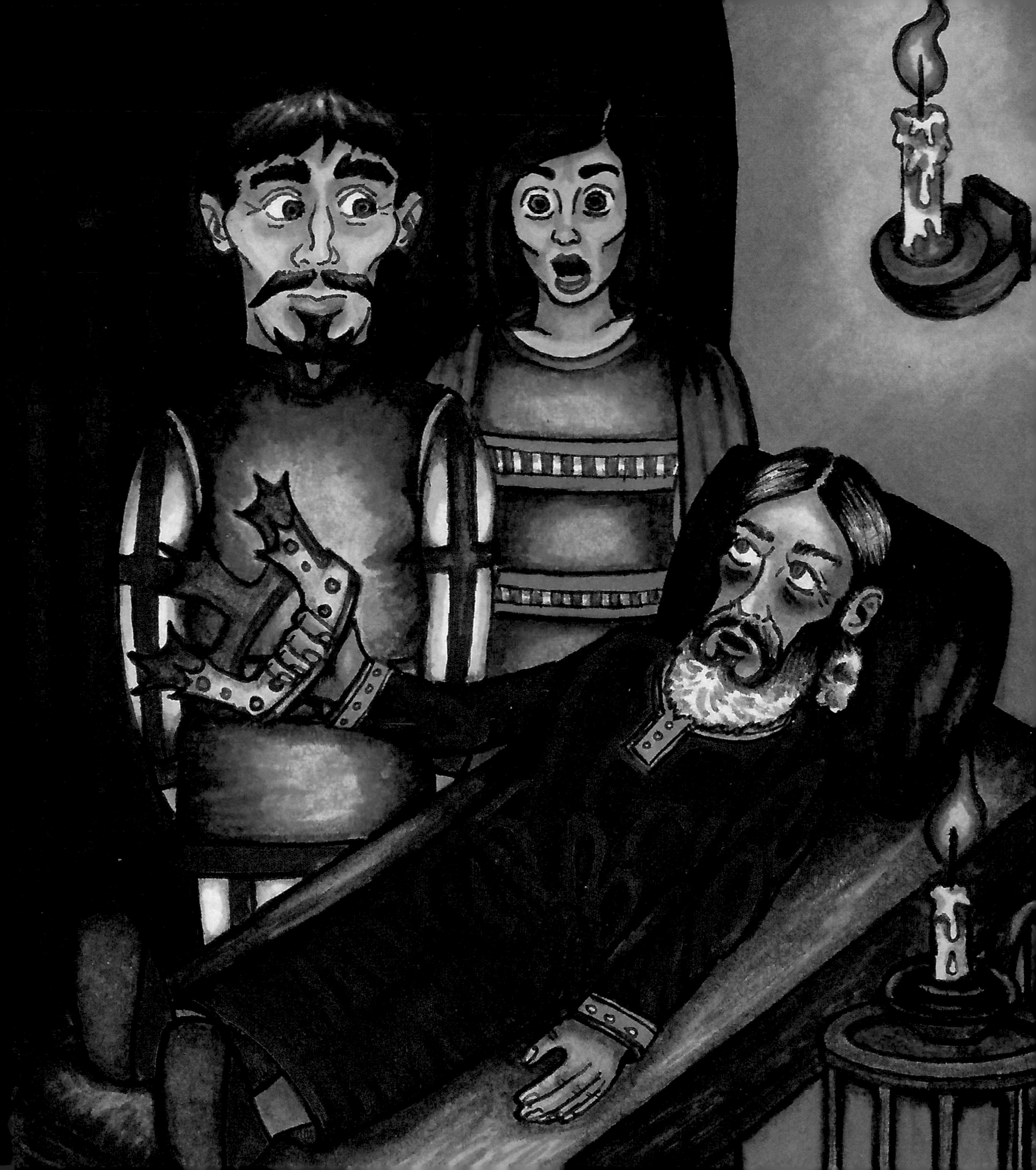

The second man was Harold Godwinson. He had big eyebrows, long hair and a moustache that flicked out at the edges. He was an Englishman and one of the most powerful people in England. He had land, riches and some strong brothers. He said that when Edward was ill in bed, Edward had promised the crown to him. Edward had told Harold Godwinson that he needed to look after England and his wife Edith, who was also Harold Godwinson's sister.

The third man was Harald Hardrada. He was a Viking. He was nearly seven foot tall and unbelievably fierce and strong. He thought that he could come to England and take the Throne. His family had been kings of England in the past. He was 15 when he started fighting in wars. Some people said he was the best warrior on earth and compared him to a thunderbolt. One of his tricks was to get birds to carry fire, so he could destroy villages. He was also already the King of Norway!

Edgar Atheling was the final person who thought he should be King. He was the nephew of Edward and a close member of the Royal family. The problem was although the English wanted him to be King, he was only fifteen years of age. He had youthful looks, he did not seem powerful and King-like but a young boy. People were worried the English Lords would boss him around to get what they wanted.

I choose Edgar, the boy of Royal Blood
I choose Harold he was chosen on Ed's death bed
I Choose Harald, Viking Kings ruled before
I Choose Willia he was Edwa Choic

Lots of people had different ideas on who should have been King. If Edward had a child (an heir), he would have been King. Lots of English people wanted an English King to rule so they choose Harold. Some wanted Edgar to be King as he was linked to Edward by blood. People in the North wanted Hardrada, the strong Viking. England was in a muddle!

EDWARD LIES HERE

Harold Godwinson knew that lots of powerful people wanted to be King. He crowned himself quickly on the day Edward had his funeral. The trouble was not over, just because Harold Godwinson wore a crown. The other people who thought they should be king had not even heard of Edward's death.

A comet came to England, staying in the sky for 15 days. A Comet is a big ball of ice and rock and turns the sky a strange colour. The English people were so scared of the Comet and it looked like there was a terrifying star in the sky. People thought that this was a sign there would be trouble for England. They were right!

ENGLAND
LONDON

Hadrada had heard that Harold Godwinson was King and was so cross. Hardrada landed in the North of England with nearly three hundred ships filled with the fiercest warriors anyone had ever seen. Hardrada thought he should be King, he was the tallest and strongest soldier on earth, and had the blood of some of the Kings before Edward. Harold Godwinson, now the King of England was still in the South. There was nobody in the North to stop this giant Viking King.

The first battle took place at Fulford, between a swamp and the River Ouse. The English people were not prepared for the attack and King Harold was not there to help them. King Harold was actually waiting in the South for William of Normandy to attack England! William was held up as the wind was not strong enough to carry his boats from France – ships then had no other source of power but the wind. The wind did not stop the Vikings who landed in the North with five thousand men. King Harold was so surprised he had not expected Hardrada to attack. He felt shocked when he saw that Hardrada was helped by Harold's own brother Tostig Godwinson. How would you feel if a member of your family decided to fight against you?

FULFORD

The Battle of Fulford was a hard fight with swords and axes. It did not start until the afternoon as the water stopped each side from getting to one another. Hardrada was clever and sent his best men round the back of the English fighters once the tide had gone out. They would be surrounded. The wild Viking King Hardrada won the battle by breaking through the English line. Hardrada's army broke through the English army with axes. Some Saxons tried to escape by swimming down the river. The bodies of the English formed a human walkway, so the Vikings didn't even get their boots muddy in the marshland. The Viking Hardrada sat smugly in York. The superhero warrior had won the North of England.

On hearing the news and seeing the bonfires. Harold Godwinson rushed to meet Hardrada; he marched all day and night for five days not allowing his men to rest. He managed to get from the South to the North in record time. Hardrada was so shocked to see Harold Godwinson. No one thought that Harold would get there that fast. Harold had been clever and his army had almost jogged from the South to the North of England. It was now Hardrada who was not ready for another battle.

NORTH

Although Harold got to the North quickly, Hardrada was silly. It was a scorching hot day, and he had left some of his weapons and armour on the boat. He even left some of his men behind to guard the ships. Being strong was not the only important thing. Only one of Hardrada's soldiers spotted the King's men, he was a Berserker. A huge Viking warrior wearing a horned helmet. He was incredibly strong and had taken a potion to make him stronger. The Berserker stood against the whole of the English army - a total of fifteen thousand men.

The bridge was the only thing that was stopping the English getting to Hardrada. The Berserker rushed to the drawbridge to stop the English from crossing and stood in their way. He killed forty Englishmen all on his own, he was fierce. One sneaky English soldier floated under the bridge and speared the Berserker near his bottom. The Berserker fell, to the floor, he was hurt. The English Army could now run over the bridge and fight against Hardrada. People said that Hardrada should run away but he said no, this strong Viking would stand and fight.

It was a hard fight, but Hardrada who was missing his armour and was cornered by the Saxons, lost the battle. He was deathly pale when he saw Harold's army. The strongest warrior that had ever walked on earth, had been beaten. He was killed with an arrow to the throat, as was Harold's brother Tostig. Harold was so happy that he had saved England from Hardrada and the Vikings. He had done the impossible! However things were not that simple.

SAXONS
BRIDGE

William had been waiting a long time to come to England. He had not had much luck with the weather (remember the winds weren't strong enough to push him across from France). However, his delay would turn out to be very lucky. Firstly, he had had lots of time to get ready. He even managed to get horses on to his ships and a flat pack castle. William landed at the most perfect of times. Harold had just fought against Hardrada. He was not as ready to fight another battle so quickly. He was also stuck in the North of England and William was in the South.

Harold heard the awful news that William had landed near Hastings with seven hundred ships and two thousand horses. He had no choice but to race back to the South of England to meet him. Harold and his men were so very tired and weak. They walked from the North to the South of England after just fighting a fierce battle with Hardrada. It appeared that luck was on Williams's side rather than Harold's.

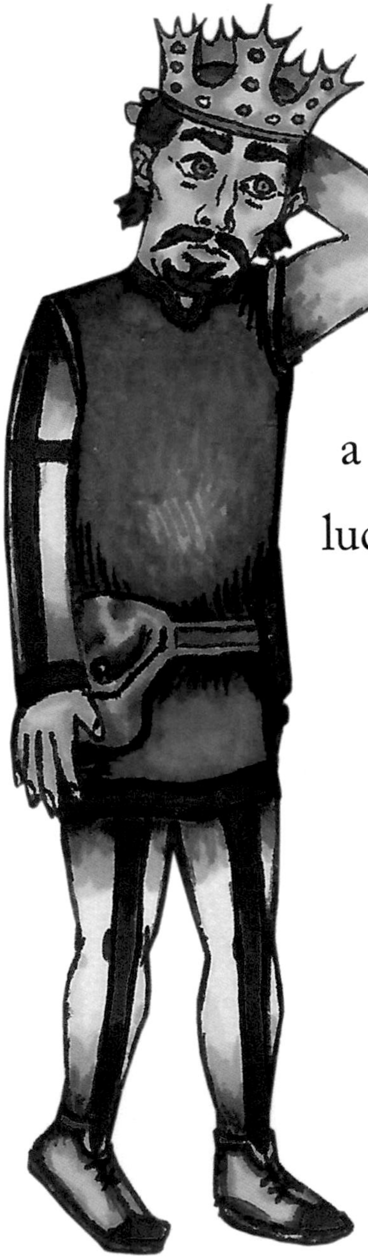

YORK
LONDON 200m

Harold was tough although very tired he did not give up. He had to be strong if he wanted to stay King of England. Harold found a brilliant place to meet William at the top of Senlac Hill. It was a perfect spot, and as long as Harold stayed at the top, he could win the battle. He was like a bird; he could see everything from there. Here there would be an epic fight that would be called the Battle of Hastings.

The trumpet blew, and the arrows filled the sky like needles. This may have been the first time the English had seen arrows in battle. The ground shook, the air roared, and the wind whistled sending both army banners high in the sky. The noise of the battle was ear-splitting, the clanging of metal, the roar of footsteps, the shouts of soldiers and the drumming of shields. The Battle of Hastings would be one of the scariest battles England would ever see. Two of the most famous armies were meeting one another.

The Battle of Hastings would last for many hours. Harold showed he was smart by making all of his men stand together shoulder to shoulder. The soldiers were holding their shield so tightly spaced, they formed a human wall. William could not get his arrows through. Harold was doing well because he was at the top of the hill with a firm shield wall. Williams's horses could not climb up the hill, and the arrows couldn't reach the soldiers at the top.

William of Normandy suddenly had an idea to trick Harold and his men. The Normans started to run down the hill. Harold's men stupidly thought they had won the battle and chased after the Norman soldiers, running down the hill. Harold was in big trouble; the human shield wall had broken. William was winning! Harold's men should never have left the best spot on the hill. Harold could not get them back as he was a king that fought alongside his men on foot.

The battle that had lasted all day ended when an arrow shot Harold through his eye. The Norman King William was the winner. As the sun came up, they saw that it seemed the Earth was bleeding. William had won the Battle of Hastings and would be called 'William the Conqueror'. What would you like to be called if you won a famous battle?

Although William had won the famous Battle of Hastings, he had not yet won the war against the English. He had to get to London from Hastings and take the City. People in London were preparing to fight William. William was smart, he kept his soldiers in Hastings for a week before making his move. William followed a route all around the City before finally entering London. He took all the towns on route and made the powerful Earls bow to him. London was surrounded and William entered the city.

England had a new Norman King who was crowned on Christmas Day. This did not happen without drama. Williams's guards thought the people cheering for the new King were starting a riot. The guards suddenly started setting fire to all the buildings. People were rushing out of the church to save their houses. William was very pale and was crowned just in time by a bishop, they were the only ones left in the church.

SAXONS KEEP OUT!
TOWER OF LONDON UNDER CONSTRUCTION

RESERVED
FOR QUEEN
MATILDA

Shortly after the mix-up, the most famous castle of all was built – what we call the Tower of London. This was made to keep William safe and show he was in charge. The Castle was huge and no one in England had seen anything like it before. People were pretty scared of the tower that had eyes on everyone. The Tower of London can be seen on the River Thames today. Have you been there?

William did not rule alone, he crowned his wife Matilda too. Matilda would take charge after William. Matilda was a very short woman and very beautiful but rocked as a queen! She made decisions quickly and carefully took care of things when William was away. He was after all King in two countries. Matilda was trusted, she bought charm to the court, and she did not care if people liked her. Matilda really made William work hard to get her hand in marriage. William loved her from her head to her

You choose:

Who do you think should have been king?

What do you think Edward should have done before he died?

What would you have chosen to take from the ship if you were Harald Hardrada?

What weapon would you choose to fight with?

What do you think was the most important item for William was take to England?

Would you have chosen to build a castle?

What would you choose to protect your castle?

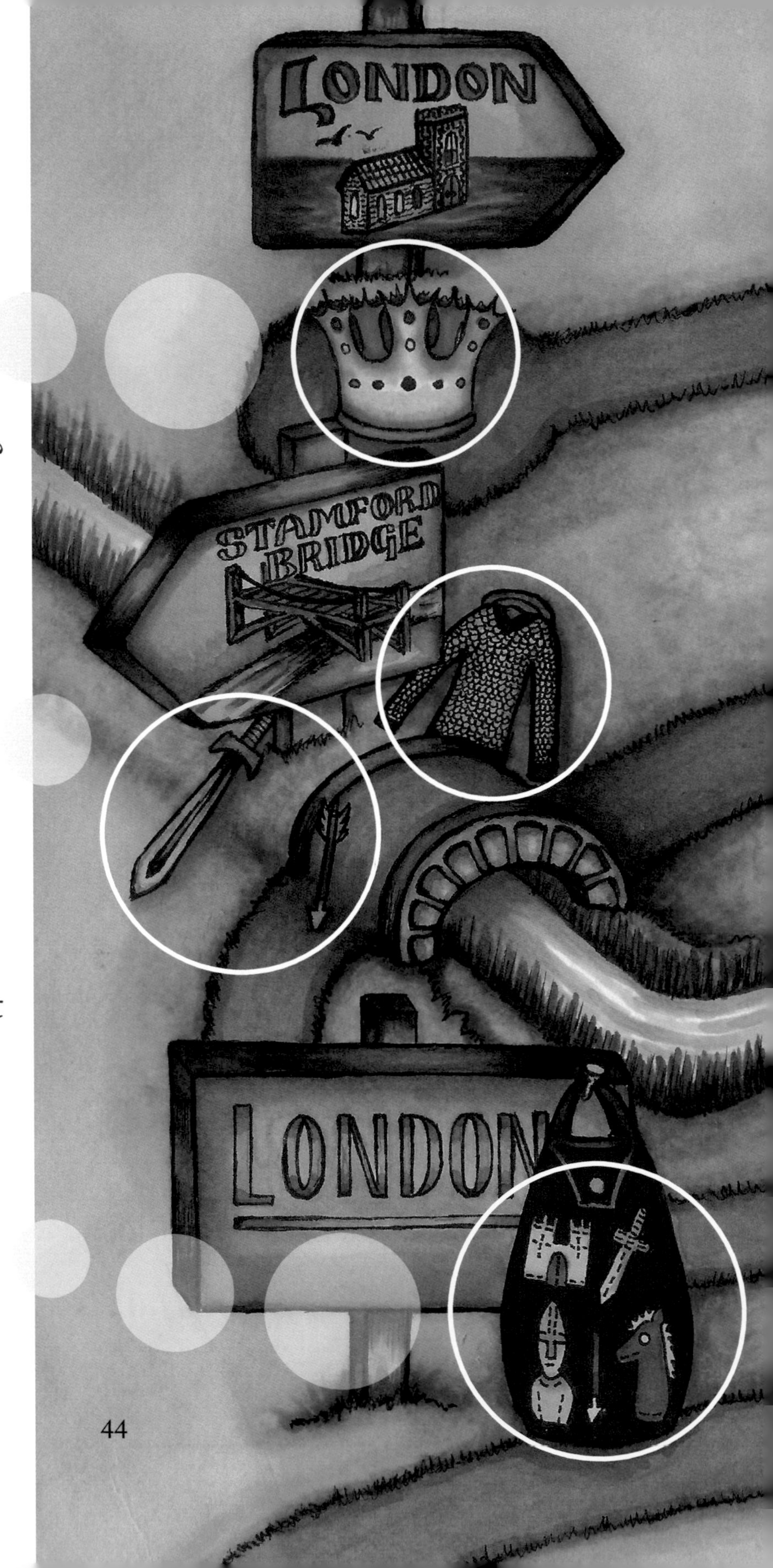

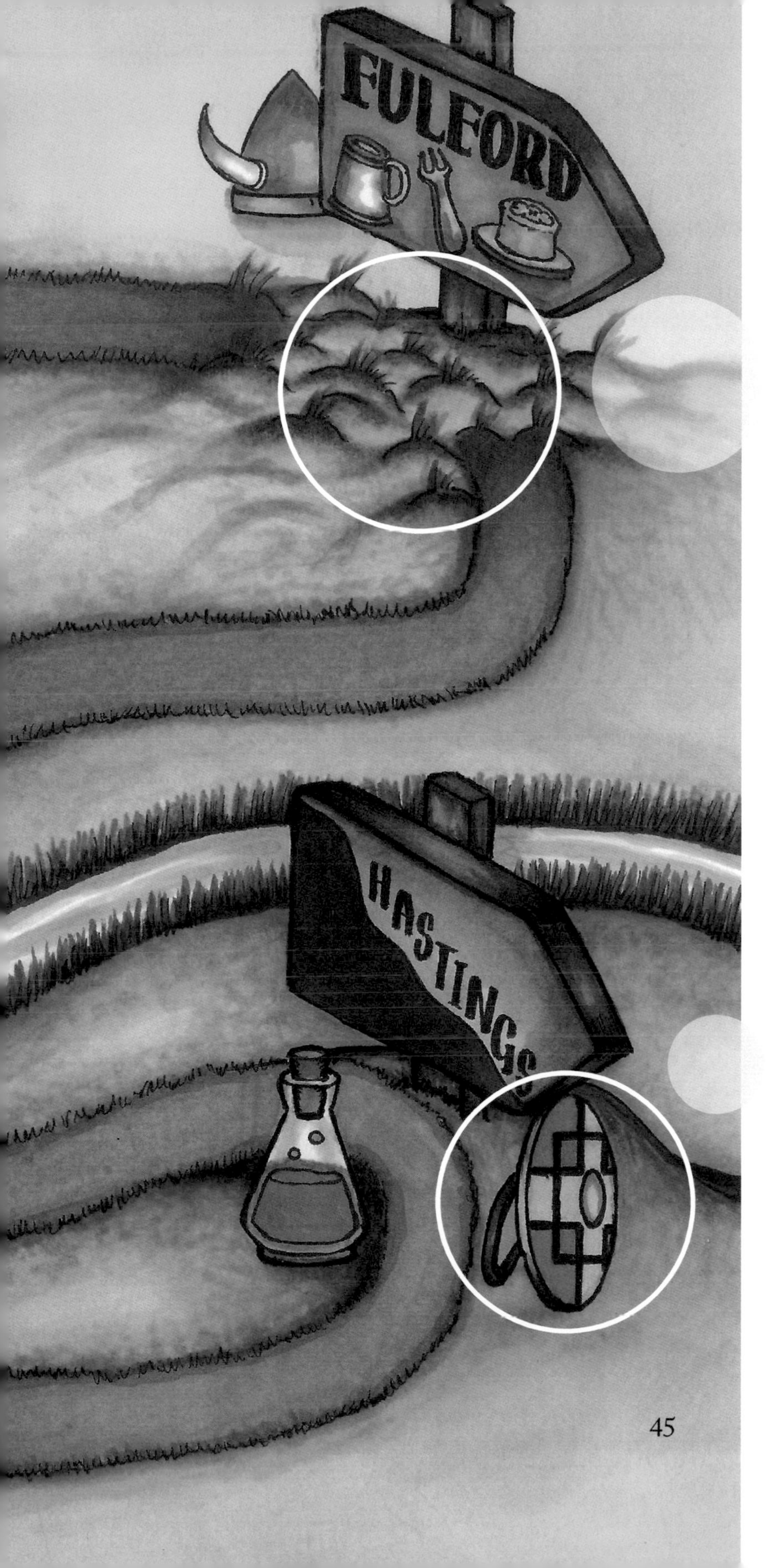

What would you choose to do if you were an English soldier at Fulford?

How would you have celebrated winning the battle?

What shield would you choose?

Would you have chosen to wait rather than fight William straightaway?

What would you choose to say to your soldiers?

The Battle of Hastings, is one of the most important battles in British history. It changed England in so many different ways. There are many lessons from this story; people should not make promises to lots of people and that being smart is just as important as being strong. That sometimes it is important to be patient and even when things look really bad you should never give up. You now have your Little Historian badge! History is for sharing, tell everyone the story of the most epic battle England has ever seen!

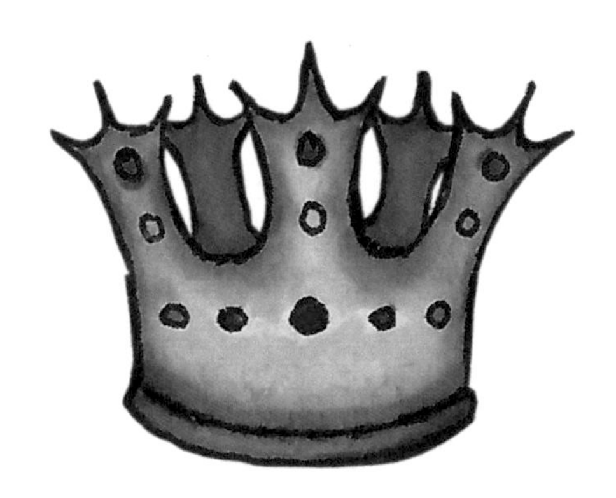